YOUR KNOWLEDGE HAS VALUE

Bibliographic information published by the German National Library:

The German National Library lists this publication in the National Bibliography; detailed bibliographic data are available on the Internet at http://dnb.dnb.de .

Imprint:

Copyright © 2016 GRIN Verlag, Open Publishing GmbH
Print and binding: Books on Demand GmbH, Norderstedt Germany
ISBN: 978-3-668-16969-2

This book at GRIN:

http://www.grin.com/en/e-book/316999/focus-groups-as-a-method-for-product-development-the-funeral-market-in

Anna Lena Bischoff

**Focus Groups as a method for product development.
The funeral market in Sweden**

GRIN Publishing

GRIN - Your knowledge has value

Since its foundation in 1998, GRIN has specialized in publishing academic texts by students, college teachers and other academics as e-book and printed book. The website www.grin.com is an ideal platform for presenting term papers, final papers, scientific essays, dissertations and specialist books.

Visit us on the internet:

http://www.grin.com/

http://www.facebook.com/grincom

http://www.twitter.com/grin_com

Contents

1. Introduction _____ 1
   1.1. Background case company_____ 2
   1.2. Results from module 2-design and module 3-engineering_____ 2

2. Theoretical framework for business methods _____ 2
   Procedure when conducting a focus group _____ 2
   Advantages and disadvantages of focus groups _____ 3

3. Empirical data collection_____ 4
   3.1. Secondary research _____ 4
   The funeral market _____4

   The funeral market in Sweden _____ 4

   Process from death to burial _____5

   3.2. Focus groups _____5

   Test focus group with students _____ 5

   Focus group with relevant customer _____ 6

   Relevant information gathered from the focus group._____ 6

   3.3. Interview with funeral home _____7

4. Analysis of the methodology_____ 8
   4.1. Critical evaluation of the method focus group_____ 8
   4.2. Critical evaluation of the method interview_____ 9

5. Conclusion_____ 10

6. Appendix _____ 11
   6.1. Table of Figures _____11
   6.2. Design Brief of The case company, including company description ____12
   6.3. Survey results from the test focus group _____ 14
   6.4. Focus group questions _____ 26
   6.5. Survey results from the focus group _____ 29
   6.6. Interview questions with the funeral company and survey results _____ 30
   6.7. Bibliography _____ 32

1. Introduction

This report is about the business methods. The report is based on the achievements acquired in the last modules. Suitable methods are needed in the business module to help the team move forward in their product development process.

Currently, the team has developed several concepts with different connection types and design styles. However, the team has no idea whether others will like this product. Without such awareness, the team would be blind to see the potential risks and shortages in the project. Thus one method is introduced to make the team aware of how potential clients or companies think about this product. The method described is a focus group. It is introduced in more detail in this paper to discuss the advantages and few disadvantages it contains.

In a focus group different target customers are gathered to discuss their views about the product's materials, the designs and whether they would purchase this product or not. If they are not interested in buying the product it is of value for the team to know, what influenced their decisions. Since this is a very special product, not only the views of potential customers are of interest, but also the knowledge and experience of experts, such as funeral companies. Therefore an interview was conducted with a funeral company to validate customer opinions.

For detailed information about the discussed company and design brief refer to ""Design Brief including company description 4.1".

1.1. Background case company

This project is conducted with a papermill. It is a local Swedish company that has a more than 200 year tradition of making stable, high quality paper products such as boxes and cardboard suitcases. Although the company has a glorious history selling their luxury paper products to all over Scandinavia, they are currently struggling to place their products on the market. The company went bankrupt several times throughout their history and managed to successfully restart from scratch. Today the case company is looking for a new innovative business idea to successfully re-enter the market of paper-based products.

1.2. Results from module 2-design and module 3-engineering

Throughout module 2 – design, the proposed idea by the case company to create a line of home office accessories was discussed and challenged. After detecting that the home office market offers little potential and would put the case company at high risk of failure, it was decided to take another approach. Ideas around the material of fiber board were discussed. Finally the concept of luxurious packaging was embraced. However, a specification of what to package was missing. The result was to package events instead of consumer goods. Several events that have a high impact on individuals due to either their life changing or traditional meaning were debated such as Christmas, weddings, birth of a baby and funerals. The project team decided to continue their work with fiber board based coffins. The decision was taken because of its innovative appeal, possibilities to discover a highly sustainable funeral solution and enter a market that offers exploration potential.

In module 3 the concept was developed in detail. A prototype was produced and the material of fiber board explored. Furthermore, the cost of material and manufacturing the coffin was derived.

2. Theoretical framework for business methods

In this chapter the method of focus groups is described as basic framework for this part of the project. The method is then critically evaluated regarding their applicability to the project.

A focus group is a method that involves participants in a discussion around a specific topic. It is often used to validate collected information .It makes use of group dynamics while protecting the individual's opinion .

Procedure when conducting a focus group

Focus groups can be conducted in small as well as large groups. Threlfall recommends to have 10-12-participants. This is due the fact that not everyone who signed up for the focus group will come. It is discussed whether a group should be diverse or homogenous among different authors. A homogenous group helps to compare the collected data from the focus group easier. Participants of a homogenous group share the same characteristics and have an easier understanding of each other's views. This can lead to more lively discussions. On the other hand diverse groups will be more confrontational and generate unexpected, diverse opinions . However, the quality of data might suffer when the group is too diverse.

Further points to consider when conducting a focus group is who to invite. When choosing the target group for the focus group, it is important to have participants that care about the topic and are interested to discuss it . Ideally they can identify themselves with the topic. It is necessary to consider potential users of the discussed product or service as participants. Kitzinger claims that it is of advantage to invite a group of friends as they can relate to each other's believes more quickly. Furthermore they will feel more comfortable to share their ideas since there is no group hierarchy with one dominant person.

To create a participatory atmosphere sessions should be comfortable and relaxed . The moderator can create a less formal setting by arranging the chairs and mixing researchers with participants instead of having one dominant person in front. At the beginning of the session the to be discussed topic should be explained by the facilitator . The moderator should guide the discussion, but not interfere too much and influence participant's opinions . To increase the discussion flow the moderator should adapt to the participants and balance their contribution. It needs to be clear that participants are equally important and work together, not against each other . An interview guide can help the moderator not to lose track of the goal of the focus group and intervene when necessary . Depending of the mixture of participants questions in the interview guide will differ. They should be open-ended and stimulate the discussion .

Participant's anecdotes and experiences can be a rich source of information to researchers. The participants should not hesitate to give long answers and have a more natural conversation than an interview .

Conflicts in focus groups might occur as well as topics that are touchy and taboos .When choosing the participants, it´s important to consider that the discussion can bring private topics and they should feel comfortable to share them just as much as being comfortable not to share their private information.

As during the focus group there are so many viewpoints and topics that will be touched it is impossible to memorize all that information. To make use of the data, it should be documented . Kitzinger suggest to tape or record the focus group.

Advantages and disadvantages of focus groups
An advantage of focus groups is the diverse insight into a topic and new thought provoking ideas . It can create a stimulus for the researcher to move forward. The speed and flexibility a focus group offers is hard to find in other research methods . Focus groups can be a source where ideas that no one has thought of before are explored and unknown perspectives are discussed . In a group, conversations get a different flow in comparison to an interview. The discussion gets its own dynamic and interaction .

If a moderator is not experienced enough to lead a focus group in a way to get the data from the conversation that is appropriate, it might become more of an interview than discussion. Furthermore if the researcher is unexperienced and does not know how to make the collected data relevant for the project, the focus group becomes useless .

Focus groups are critiqued for their artificial set-up . To discuss a topic in a relaxed atmosphere might be different from real life were decisions are taken ion impulse or under stress.

Researchers need to be aware that opinions in a focus group might influence each other . Moreover they should not be certain that an opinion is an individual points of view or whether it can be generalized. A focus group is too small and specialized to represent society or generalize a majorities' opinion.

3. Empirical data collection

This chapter documents how data was collected and which information was collected.

3.1.   Secondary research

The funeral market
The funeral market is facing new challenges as corpses seem to take more time to decrease due to the human diet that has changed over the last centuries as well as the demand for looser regulations. This is especially true for the place of burial which is currently highly regulated in most European countries. However there is an interest to open the regulations and allow further places such as private gardens for burial.

Besides these factors there is demand for less expensive but dignifying ways to bury the dead. The most expensive cost of a funeral is the casket, which on average has a mark-up of 289% from wholesale to retail, but sometimes can be much higher . This demand asks for new materials for urns and coffins. One step towards the future is that the European commission has registered biofiber composite to the European funeral industry.

The funeral market in Sweden
The total European market size is ~4.600.000 coffins/year . The funeral market is one with a prosperous future due to shifts in demographics. Currently 20% of the Swedish population is over 65 years old .

80% of the deaths are cremated in Sweden . Cremation can take place either in an urn or a coffin. Swedish citizens are entitled to a gravesite for 25 years once they have paid the burial fee. Gravesites can only places that are publically determined as such places such as cemeteries. The fee includes further services such as transportation, cremation and site opening. . In 2012 the fee was 0,22% of taxable income .

Legal matters are regulated in the "Begravningslag (1990:1144)" The law regulates e.g. that burned ashes have to be buried within a year after cremation, or that a gravesite needs to be freed for the next corpse after 25 years. There are no regulations concerning the corpse contaminating the soil as the ide is "dust to dust".

Process from death to burial
The dead body is directly transported to the hospital morgue . Funeral homes do not take care of the corpse. Most funeral homes in Sweden are family owned.

The funeral home provides the services around the funeral ceremony. Unique to Sweden is the "vita arkivet", which is a platform that allows people prior to their death to plan their burial. Once they decease the information is made available to relatives.

Embalming is very uncommon in Sweden whereas cremation has become much more popular during the last couple of years.

When an earth burial is conducted the coffin will be released into the ground after the ceremony. The coffin is carried by six people .

3.2. Focus groups

The first step in setting up the focus group was to decide the number of focus groups, participants and actual set up. It was decided to have a test-run focus group with students and a focus group with participants that are more concerned about the topic.

 The project team had to find out which information is needed to collect relevant data to go forward in the product development process.

Test focus group with students
The students participating in the test run were assigned to the project team. They were four students studying for a Master degree in Entrepreneurship. The focus group was set up for two hours.

Questions that would concern the end-user were composed for an interview guide and small survey. These questions included different perspectives such as the participant's judgment on business aspects as well as their opinion as a potential customer. The questions and survey answers can be found in "6.5Survey results from the test focus group". It also needed to be considered how to introduce the topic as it is a sensitive subject and not many people think about it unless confronted with the situation of death.

The company The case company was introduced as a papermill. The aim was to concentrate on the material first to open up the participants mind. The project team asked for thoughts and ideas around cardboard. The participant's ideas mirrored the process the project team went through by developing ideas for cardboard products such as furniture, packaging or building material. The project team revealed then that fiber board is one of the boundaries for developing a product for The case company. Next, the concrete topic to make cardboard coffins was introduced. The participants discussed advantages such as sustainability, price, etc. and disadvantages. They were interested in the customizing possibility of the product. One of the participants shared personal experiences from a funeral and that she remembered how costly it was.

Competitor products and the Solidworks sketch were shown to take the conversation to the next level. Here the different styles of coffins became visible. The students preferred a more traditional look.

In the end the students were handed a survey to answer questions around cardboard coffins and feedback for improvement of the process for the next focus group.

Focus group with relevant customer
Given that broach the subject of coffin is sensitive, the decision to do the focus group with participants that know each other was made. The decision was to ask a family member, which lead to doing the focus group with one of the group member's grand-mother and her two friends to participate as focus group.

The focus group took place at the relative's apartment around a fika. It was important that the participants were in a familiar place to be comfortable to share their experience and opinion.

A cozy atmosphere was set up to help the three participants to feel at ease to talk about the topic.

From the previous focus group it was understood that students are not relevant regarding the current concept, because it was difficult for them to imagine the coffin they would choose when being confronted with the situation of funerals. Hence, it seemed more appropriate to discuss the topic with experienced consumers. They are closer to the topic of burials and have experience with being confronted to choose a coffin. Elisa, one of the group members, served as moderator when conducting the focus group. She decided to start from a general aspect by talking about the funerals, to finish with the specific product that is being developed.

To begin the session, the company was introduced and their products were shown to the participants. Then the topic of funerals was approached. The discussion started when the participants shared their experience with funerals and how they chose or would choose a coffin. Afterwards, the conversation was oriented around the concept of cardboard coffin. Next, some products of cardboard coffin competitors were compared to analyze what is appreciated or not about the coffins. Especially, aspects for the fiberboard coffin were discussed. The last part of the focus group was to show the fiberboard coffin developed for The case company. The aim was to have their opinion about the product to know how it can be improved.

Relevant information gathered from the focus group.
The first thing they said and agreed on is that they don't want an expensive coffin. They consider it a waste of money. Furthermore, they pointed out that cremation is more appealing to them. If the coffin is not good looking, they would use a beautiful cover during the ceremony. They don't consider the

coffin as the most important piece of the funeral. They are more concerned about the music and the place. One of the participants insisted on the fact that her coffin should be cheap, eco-friendly and simple. They are not interested in decoration for their coffin; however a traditional and neutral look is important for them.

When some of the competitors' products were presented, they disliked the coffins with flowers and a lot of color.

One of the participants shared her experience when she had to choose a coffin for her husband. She bought an expensive coffin, she explained, as she wanted the best for him. For her being generous was a way to show that he was important to her. Nevertheless, they said that the money shouldn't be wasted on the coffin but rather put into the other parts of the ceremony.

Being inhumed or cremated in a fiberboard coffin is completely conceivable for the three participants. This concept is very appreciated by them, as it's a cheap and eco-friendly alternative to wood coffins. When talking about the product developed for The case company, two of the participants appreciated the design. The third participant thought that the handles looked too "trivial".

As a conclusion, it can be mentioned that they are seeing their funeral as a way to celebrate their life because "death is the only certain thing in life"

The results from the survey can be found in "6.3Survey results from the focus group".

3.3.   Interview with funeral home

The interview took place on the 17th December at E.N. Funeral services offices. A semi-structured list of open questions was prepared in advance. The interviewee has worked at the funeral service for 25 years with a wide knowledge of the market. To start the interview he shared information about the funeral market. It was found that the Swedish market has changed due to a higher live expectancy in the Swedish population and demographic shifts.

The Swedish market offers lower prices on coffins in comparison with U.S. Moreover, coffins were adapted to increasing obesity. Coffins are not the priority when arranging the funeral, indeed the first concern is the place, priest and music. The main criteria for choosing the coffins are price, color and appearance. The bestseller coffin is one of the lower price ranges, with a price of 4700Kr. However, the cheapest coffin costs 3000kr. Coffins that are not traditional are hard to sell. An example is that E. N. tried to sell coffins from Jacob Jensen and it has been a failure in sale due to the lack of traditional appearance and too high price. The interviewee recalled that the cardboard coffins were developed 25 years ago by "Rydens". Nevertheless, the product has not been launched and will be released spring/summer 2016. Nowadays, customers are more Eco-aware, therefore E. N. offers eco-Friendly coffins. He expressed a positive perspective on this project.

More information was required about the funeral process. 85% of the customers demand cremation. The procedure for cremation is the burning of the corpse at 1000 degree. Nothing is left apart from the metal pieces.

Law regulates that after 25 years the leftovers of the coffins and body should be dug out from the ground.

The questions and survey results with E. N. can be found in "6.4 Interview questions with the funeral company and survey results".

4. Analysis of the methodology

After having set the methodological framework in chapter two, method of a focus group will be critically evaluated.

4.1. Critical evaluation of the method focus group

In the beginning a test focus group was held to gather experience, refine questions and set-up. The test focus group helped to test whether the questions asked and the set up was applicable to gather valid data. It was found that the questions were precise and to the point. A survey conducted at the end of the session aided to give weight to different opinions on different components of the product. The questionnaire showed clear results. However, during the discussion it became clear that the test focus group did not consist of the proper target group. Therefore it was chosen to approach a more applicable target group in the conduction of the real focus group. The questionnaire and guiding questions for the moderator of the focus group would only be adjusted slightly for the real focus group.

The focus group was conducted in a small group. Since Threlfall (1999) suggest a minimum of 10 participants, it needs to be considered that the focus group might not show representative results. Focus groups can be conducted in small as well as large groups.

Furthermore a homogenous group was chosen with similar social and demographic structure. It was found that the data is easier to compare and that the participants have an easier understanding of each other just as Grudens-Schuck, Allen, & Larson suggested. The participants could identify themselves with the topic easily as they had experience with the burial of a beloved person and are potential future customers of the product.

To create a comfortable atmosphere the focus group was held over a fika and Elisa served as moderator. She used an interview guide which was developed by the team members and further refined after the focus group testrun. The interview guide helped to stay focused and Elisa was able to use her moderator experience gathered during the testrun.

Conflicts in the group occurred in the form of differences in opinion. However, participants felt comfortable enough to discuss these differences due to their close relationship as friends.

The advantage of the focus group with Elisa's grandmother and her friends was the diverse and close insight on the participant's opinion on a sensitive topic. This focus group gave good results in the questionnaire and a lot of input for the product. They brought up ideas that were not considered before e.g. that the coffin can be covered with a beautiful duvet if it is not good-looking.

The focus group confirmed that the concept of creating coffins at a fraction of the price of a regular wood coffin seems attractive. Fiber board can prove a valuable alternative material as long as looks are not compromised.

It shouldn't be forgotten that in this case the artificial set-up of the focus group is nowhere close to real life. In real life the decision to choose a coffin is a purchase that might happen very few times in a person's life and is done under high stress. The focus group couldn't reflect how potential customers would make their purchasing decision when under emotions and stress. Instead the focus group gave a rational and clear reflection on the topic, which might not be applicable in real life.

Also it needs to be considered that the focus group was quite small and is not representative of a whole segment of customers. It only gives insight in some thoughts and ideas.

Therefore, it was considered that the focus group alone would not be sufficient to evaluate whether the concept is promising. To further validate the gathered information, the interview with a funeral home was conducted.

4.2.   Critical evaluation of the method interview

The interview was important as an employee has direct insights in e.g. the selling process and knows what the customer's demands are in coffins. He can give further insight on how customers react under stress and when trapped in negative emotions.

It would have been ideal to have a focus group with funeral home employees to get more than one opinion and be able to compare perceptions. Unfortunately it proved to be difficult to find a time that suited several employees. Since the insight from an employee would be so valuable, it was decided not to drop the idea and do an interview with the biggest funeral home instead. The interview was necessary to understand the procedures and process around a funeral better and equip the project team with more knowledge about the market. Therefore this method had a different emphasis than the focus group.

The information received was more focused whether the concept itself would be accepted in the market and whether there is already competition for fiber board coffins existing. This information could not have been provided by the focus group as they lacked market knowledge.

The interview proved very valuable as further knowledge source.

5. Conclusion

Focus groups can be a very valuable method when customer insights are needed. However, it shouldn't be forgotten that one focus group only represents a little, restricted insights of the average customer. Therefore it should be considered to have several focus groups or use further methods to validate the data such as interviews. Only the combination of interview and focus group helped to critically reflect the opinions of both groups. Both groups agreed that the price was the most important aspect in the purchasing decision, followed by the wish for a traditional design.

A better approach would have been to use focus groups early on in the development process to get an understanding whether the general direction of the concept would be accepted by customers or which product features should be adjusted. The focus group can then lead as a guide with the company deciding how much room they want to give to the focus group's opinion in their product development.

Focus groups are always very personal and not objective. Participants in an anonymous survey might be braver to state their opinion. This might be especially true to sensitive subjects were it can be difficult for participants to discuss their feelings openly. On the other hand insights are not a s personal and deep.

In this case, the method seemed applicable and gave valuable data, but it can only be considered critically in the product development process. Especially with such a sensitive topic it would have been good to have more time to dedicate to further focus groups or a larger survey.

6. Appendix

6.1.   Table of Figures

Figure 1: Survey results from the focus group 29

Figure 2: Questions and survey results with the funeral company 30

Figure 3: Wood samples for coffins 31

6.2.   Design Brief of The case company, including company description

This is just a suggestion of questions formulations that you can work with. We can together talk about if your background our earlier experience would be better to focus on some of this questions and also what is reasonable for your timeline. It is important that you all feel inspired.

Objective of the project

What does the project requires from the business perspective?

* How should we marketing and sale the new products. Is our idea of sell it on the web the best way to go? Create a business and marketing plan. How is our target?

* Make a suggestion/ a plan of how we should work with advertising, also a budget for this.

* Calculate how much the production cost is, row material and what should we sale it fore?

* Brand, how can we make our brand stronger?

* How can we make the production and product more cost-effective?

* How are our competitors? What can we do to stand out from them? What do we offer that they do not do, and how can we show this for our costumer?

What does the project requires from the engineering perspective?

* Construction of the box, dare to question the flat packing solution on the market today. How can we make it so easy for both in the production and also for the costumer?

* Production, can we make the production of the flat packing line more effective? Technique, machines, details.

* Sustainability, how can we work with sustainability in a better and more effective way? Also how can the customer easy separate the different

* Explore what sizes there boxes should be.

What does the project requires from the design perspective?

* Material, fiber board paper, leather and metal details.

* How is the user for this product? And how will he/she use it? What are our users' needs and how do they perceive the product. How are the different stakeholders for the project? Try to involve them in to the project.

* Sizes, investigate witch sizes our user need. How many part should there be in the collection? Shape, color, prints etc.

* A construction that holds the boxes together, how can you make it in to a detail? Work with construction, function and shape..

* If a manual is necessary for the costumer to put the boxes together, make a manual that fit the graphic profile and is easy to understand (illustrated).

* Sustainability, how can sustainability be a part of this project? Material, construction, etc.

Our company's wishes, feelings and expectations

* Our wishes are that your group creates something that fits both the private and the public sector.

* It is important that it is a clear line between all different elements. Try to involved and be inspired of our key word is: History, craftsmanship and Sweden.

Timing and approvals

This is given by us according to the course schedule

6.3. Survey results from the test focus group

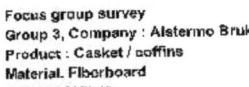

Focus group survey
Group 3, Company : Alstermo Bruk
Product : Casket / coffins
Material. Fiberboard
3.12.2016 Växjö

The purpose of this short survey is to gather data from different potential user of a product in order to analyses the data in an effective way. This input and opinions will be uses for academic objectives. Answers will be treated anonymously.

Answer the following questions based on your own opinion

1. Have you attended a funeral?

Yes___ No _✗_

2. If yes, how did you perceive the importance of the coffin during the ceremony?

3. What do you think is the main criteria of people when choosing a casket (e.g. price, look, sustainability...)?

looks + price

4. Have you thought about what your funeral / a close relatives funeral should look like?

yes

5. If so how? What is the most important to you?

to value the person life, a decease by personality. Some that will be remembered

6. What would be your personal criteria when choosing a casket?

looks + price.

7. Which are the most relevant features in order to make a coffin?

design

8. Have you heard of fiberboard coffins?

yes

14

9. What do you associate with fiber board?

[handwritten, illegible]

10. What do you associate with fiber board?

[handwritten, illegible]

11. How do you perceive fiberboard coffins?

[handwritten, illegible]

12. Why would you buy it or not buy it?

[handwritten, illegible]

13. Are you familiar with the fiberboard coffin concept? What do you think about it?

[handwritten, illegible]

14. As a customer are you concerned about being eco-aware?

[handwritten, illegible]

15. Would you be interested in customize your coffin or do you prefer neutrality?

[handwritten, illegible]

16. What do you think of the stability of fiberboard?

[handwritten, illegible]

17. Have you bought fiberboard containers?

[handwritten, illegible]

18. Which way you prefer to buy goods? Market or online?

[handwritten] market

19. What would be important to you when buying a coffin?

Criterias	Irrelevant				Relevant
	1	2	3	4	5
Color			X		
Sustainability		X			
Appearance/Aesthetics					X
Customer Rating			X		
Recommendation by Relatives		X			
Price					X
Craftmanship				X	
Material		X			
Individualization			X		

Focus group survey
Group 3, Company : Alstermo Bruk
Product : Casket / coffins
Material. Fiberboard
3.12.2015 Växjö

The purpose of this short survey is to gather data from different potential user of a product in order to analyses the data in an effective way. This input and opinions will be uses for academic objectives. Answers will be treated anonymously.

Answer the following questions based on your own opinion

1. Have you attended a funeral?

    Yes _X_   No _____

2. If yes, how did you perceive the importance of the coffin during the ceremony?
    [handwritten, illegible]

3. What do you think is the main criteria of people when choosing a casket (e.g. price, look, sustainability...)?
    [handwritten, illegible]

4. Have you thought about what your funeral/ a close relatives funeral should look like?
    [handwritten, illegible] yes

5. If so how? What is the most important to you?
    [handwritten, illegible]

6. What would be your personal criteria when choosing a casket?
    [handwritten, illegible]

7. Which are the most relevant features in order to make a coffin?
    [handwritten, illegible]

8. Have you heard of fiber board coffins?
    [handwritten, illegible]

9. What do you associate with fiber board?

[handwritten, illegible]

10. What do you associate with fiber board?

[handwritten, illegible]

11. How do you perceive fiberboard coffins ?

[handwritten, illegible]

12. Why would you buy it or not buy it?

[handwritten, illegible]

13. Are you familiar with the fiberboard coffin concept? What do you think about it?

[handwritten, illegible]

14. As a customer are you concerned about being eco-aware?

[handwritten, illegible]

15. Would you be interested in customize your coffin or do you prefer neutrality?

[handwritten, illegible]

16. What do you think of the stability of fiberboard?

[handwritten, illegible]

17. Have you bought fiberboard containers?

[handwritten, illegible]

18. Which way you prefer to buy goods ? Market or online?

[handwritten] market.

19. What would be important to you when buying a coffin?

Criterias	Irrelevant				Relevant
	1	2	3	4	5
Color		X			
Sustainability					X
Appearance/Aesthetics			X		
Customs Rating					X
Recommendation by Relatives					X
Price					X
Craftmanship					X
Material					X
(Environmentality)					X

Focus group survey
Group 3, Company : Alstermo Bruk
Product : Casket / coffins
Material. Fiberboard
3.12.2015 Växjö

The purpose of this short survey is to gather data from different potential user of
a product in order to analyses the data in an effective way. This input and opinions
will be uses for academic objectives. Answers will be treated anonymously.

Answer the following questions based on your own opinion

1.   Have you attended a funeral?

Yes _✓_   No _____

2.   If yes, how did you perceive the importance of the coffin during the ceremony?

      To a certain extent, high

3.   What do you think is the main criteria of people when choosing a casket (e.g.
price, look, sustainability...)?

      price, look, quality

4.   Have you thought about what your funeral/ a close relatives funeral should look
like?

      not really

5.   If so how? What is the most important to you?

      a good funeral package

6.   What would be your personal criteria when choosing a casket?

      a simple casket

7.   Which are the most relevant features in order to make a coffin?

      a good quality durable coffin

8.   Have you heard of fiber board coffins?

      just now

20

9. What do you associate with fiber board?

furniture, boxes, photocopy

10. What do you associate with fiber board?

11. How do you perceive fiberboard coffins ?

they look good quality, Compare

12. Why would you buy it or not buy it?

availability, quality, price
(first is best)

13. Are you familiar with the fiberboard coffin concept? What do you think about it?

No; it looks good

14. As a customer are you concerned about being eco-aware?

Yes, I don't want that coffin to decompose quickly in the southern lowland.

15. Would you be interested in customize your coffin or do you prefer neutrality?

maybe customize it, or a place a family photo.

16. What do you think of the stability of fiberboard?

very important.

17. Have you bought fiberboard containers?

No.

18. Which way you prefer to buy goods ? Market or online?

depends, some cases go to the market.

19. What would be important to you when buying a coffin?

| Criterias | Irrelevant | | | | Relevant |
	1	2	3	4	5
Color					
Sustainability					
Appereance/Aesthetics					
Custome Rating					
Recomendation by Relatives					
Price					
Craftmanship					
Material					

Focus group survey
Group 3, Company : Alstermo Bruk
Product : Casket / coffins
Material. Fiberboard
3.12.2015 Växjö

The purpose of this short survey is to gather data from different potential user of
a product in order to analyses the data in an effective way. This input and opinions
will be uses for academic objectives. Answers will be treated anonymously.

Answer the following questions based on your own opinion

1. Have you attended a funeral?

Yes _✓_   No_____

2. If yes, how did you perceive the importance of the coffin during the ceremony?

Not really important, Normally respect coffin made of wood are not in a christian prayer.

3. What do you think is the main criteria of people when choosing a casket (e.g.
price, look, sustainability...)?

Price, Quality

4. Have you though about what your funeral/ a close relatives funeral should look
like?

Yes

5. If so how? What is the most important to you?

Ceremony

6. What would be your personal criteria when choosing a casket?

Not too expensive for the family

7. Which are the most relevant features in order to make a coffin?

Stable

8. Have you heard of fiber board coffins?

Not until today

23

9. What do you associate with fiber board?

(light ... and very stable)

10. What do you associate with fiber board?

11. How do you perceive fiberboard coffins?

12. Why would you buy it or not buy it?

(price and design)

13. Are you familiar with the fiberboard coffin concept? What do you think about it?

(It is a good idea. Partly to celebrate)

14. As a customer are you concerned about being eco-aware?

(No)

15. Would you be interested in customize your coffin or do you prefer neutrality?

(customized)

16. What do you think of the stability of fiberboard?

(If done correctly it shouldn't be a problem. This should be communicated)

17. Have you bought fiberboard containers?

(No)

18. Which way you prefer to buy goods? Market or online?

(Both. High priced buys at/pick a market)

19. What would be important to you when buying a coffin?

| Criterias | Irrelevant | | | | Relevant |
	1	2	3	4	5
Color				X	
Sustainability				X	
Appereance/Aesthetics				X	
Custome Rating			X		
Recomendation by Relatives		X			
Price					X
Craftmanship			X		
Material			X		
Environment(?)				X	

6.4. Focus group questions

Focus group survey
Group 3, Company : Alstermo Bruk
Product : Casket / coffins
Material. Fiberboard
18.12.2015 Växjö

The purpose of this short survey is to gather data from different potential user of a product in order to analyses the data in an effective way. This input and opinions will be uses for academic objectives. Answers will be treated anonymously.

Answer the following questions based on your own opinion

1. Are you familiar with the concept of fiber board/cardboard coffins?

Yes_____   No_____

2. What do you associate with fiber board?

3. What do you think of the stability of fiberboard?

4. Have you bought fiberboard containers?

5. How do you perceive fiberboard coffins ?

6. What do you think is the main criteria of people when choosing a casket (e.g. price, look, sustainability...)?

7. Which are the most relevant features in order to make a coffin?

8. Why would you buy it or not buy it?

9. As a customer are you concerned about being eco-aware?

10. Would you be interested in customize your coffin or do you prefer neutrality?

11. What would be important to you when buying a coffin?

Criterias	Irrelevant				Relevant
	1	2	3	4	5
Color					
Sustainability					
Appereance/Aesthetics					
Custome Rating					
Recomendation by Relatives					
Price					
Craftmanship					
Material					

6.5. Survey results from the focus group

Criterias	Irrelevant 1	2	3	4	Relevant 5
Color					X
Sustainability					X
Appereance/Aesthetics			X		
Custome Rating	X				
Recomendation by Relatives			X		
Price					X
Craftmanship					X
Material					X

Criterias	Irrelevant 1	2	3	4	Relevant 5
Color					X
Sustainability	X				
Appereance/Aesthetics				X	
Custome Rating	X				
Recomendation by Relatives	X			X	
Price				X	
Craftmanship				X	
Material				X	

Criterias	Irrelevant 1	2	3	4	Relevant 5
Color	X				
Sustainability	X				
Appereance/Aesthetics			X		
Custome Rating	X				
Recomendation by Relatives			X		
Price				X	
Craftmanship				X	
Material				X	

Figure 1: Survey results from the focus group

6.6. Interview questions with the funeral company and survey results

1. Have you seen changes in the funeral business?
2. What are the laws and regulations that are considered during the funeral and after(underground)?
3. Can you describe how the burial process works in Sweden?
4. Can people choose cremation or burial?
5. How long does the coffin stay in the ground? How many years?
6. When the coffin is cremated or the grave is opened what happens to the parts that cannot decompose such as metal?
7. What metal is used in coffins?
8. Do you sell the coffins to the customer directly or do you recommend a company?
9. What is your bestselling coffin? Do you have a picture? How much does it cost?
10. What do you think is the main criteria of people when choosing a casket (e.g. price, look, sustainability...)?
11. Are you familiar with the concept of fiber board/cardboard coffins?
12. How do you perceive fiberboard coffins? What are your thoughts?
13. Have you sold fiber board coffins to customers?
14. Have you suggested fiber board coffins, when the customer chooses its coffin?
15. Do you think your customers are eco-aware?
16. Do you think the customer is interested in customization?
17. How important is the price when deciding the coffin? What is the price range of the most common coffins?

Criteria	Irrelevant 1	2	3	4	Relevant 5
Color				X	
Sustainability					X
Appearance				X	
Customer ratings		X			
Recommendation by relatives			X		
Price					X
Craftsmanship			X		X
Material		X	X		
Customization/Individualizatio			X		
Ergonomics			X		
Weight		X			
Handling					X

individuell grades

Figure 2: Questions and survey results with the funeral company

Figure 3: Wood samples for coffins

6.7. Bibliography

Bryman, A., & Bell, E. (2011). *Business Research Methods.* OUP Oxford.

Grudens-Schuck, N., Allen, B. L., & Larson, K. (2004). Methodology: Focus Group Fundamentals. *Digital Repository @ Iowa State University.*

Kitzinger, J. (1995). Introducing focus groups. *BMJ: British Medical Journal* , 299-302.

Stokes, D., & Bergin, R. (2006). Methodology or "methodolatry"? An evaluation of focus groups and depth interviews. *Qualitative Market Reserach: An International Journal,* 26-37.

Threlfall, K. D. (1999). Using focus group as consumer research tool. *Journal of Marketing Practice: Apllied Marketing Science,* 102-105.